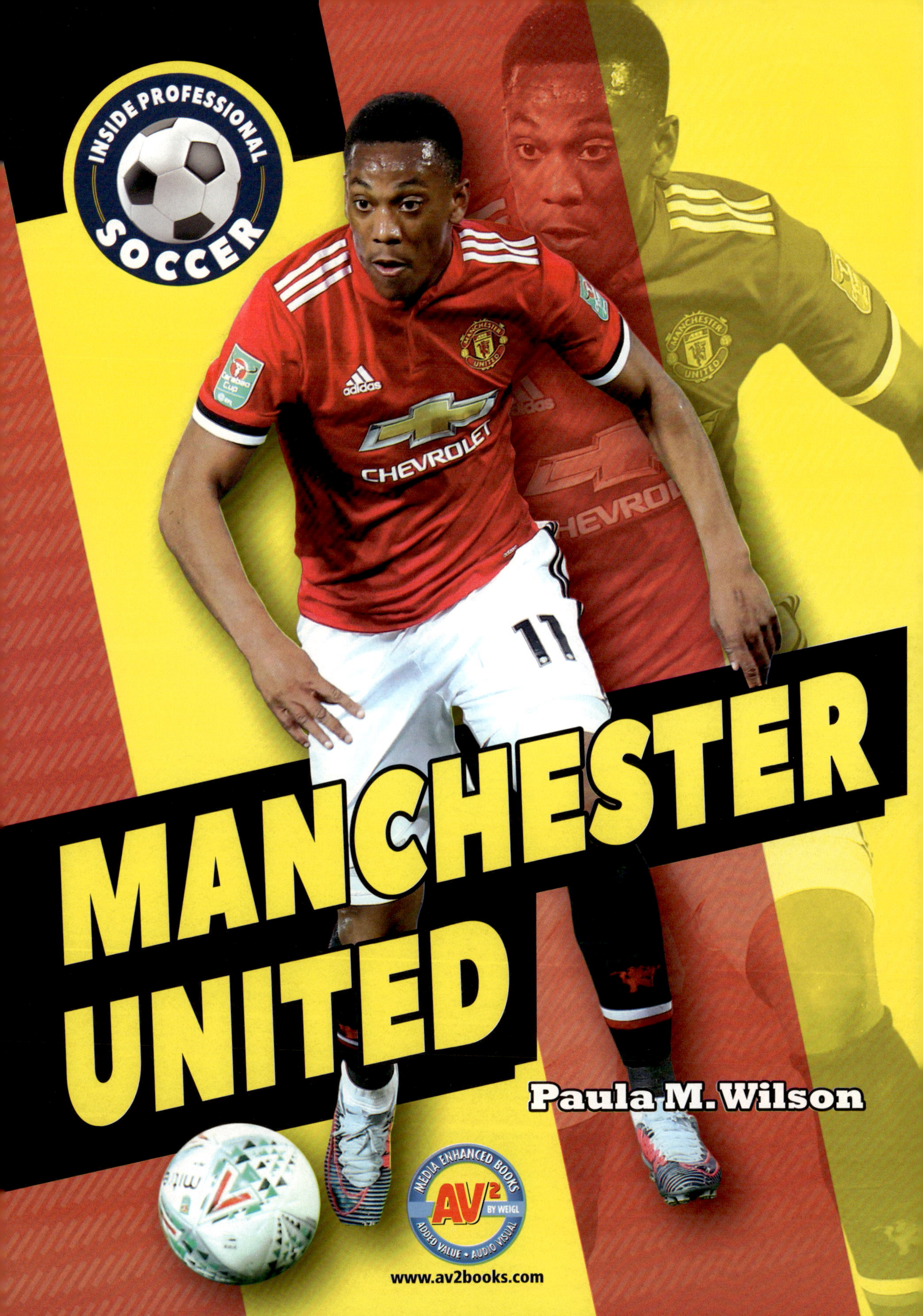
INSIDE PROFESSIONAL
SOCCER
MANCHESTER
UNITED
Paula M. Wilson
MEDIA ENHANCED BOOKS
AV2
BY WEIGL
ADDED VALUE • AUDIO VISUAL
www.av2books.com

Go to www.av2books.com, and enter this book's unique code.

BOOK CODE

AVF92842

AV² by Weigl brings you media enhanced books that support active learning.

AV² provides enriched content that supplements and complements this book. Weigl's AV² books strive to create inspired learning and engage young minds in a total learning experience.

Your AV² Media Enhanced books come alive with...

Audio
Listen to sections of the book read aloud.

Key Words
Study vocabulary, and complete a matching word activity.

Video
Watch informative video clips.

Quizzes
Test your knowledge.

Embedded Weblinks
Gain additional information for research.

Slide Show
View images and captions, and prepare a presentation.

Try This!
Complete activities and hands-on experiments.

... and much, much more!

Published by AV² by Weigl
350 5th Avenue, 59th Floor
New York, NY 10118
Website: www.av2books.com

Library of Congress Control Number: 2018930408

ISBN 978-1-4896-7778-5 (hardcover)
ISBN 978-1-4896-7779-2 (softcover)
ISBN 978-1-4896-7780-8 (multi-user eBook)

Printed in the United States of America in Brainerd, Minnesota
1 2 3 4 5 6 7 8 9 0 22 21 20 19 18

022018
120817

Project Coordinator: John Willis Designer: Terry Paulhus

Every reasonable effort has been made to trace ownership and to obtain permission to reprint copyright material. The publishers would be pleased to have any errors or omissions brought to their attention so that they may be corrected in subsequent printings.

The publisher acknowledges Getty Images and Alamy as its primary image suppliers for this title.

INSIDE PROFESSIONAL SOCCER

CONTENTS

Introduction

Manchester United is named after Manchester, England, a city in the northwest part of the country. The team is part of the English Premier League, the highest division of English soccer. The league used to be called the Football League First Division. In 1992, the group split and the new division was called the Premier League.

Most European countries, including England, call soccer "football." Soccer is a big part of the culture in England. Team loyalties go back generations. From their early years until now, Manchester United has delighted fans by winning dozens of championships, **cups**, and titles. The competition is fierce among professional soccer teams in England. However, Manchester United has been successful year after year. They have finished at the top of the Premier League more than any other team. Due to their ongoing success, Manchester United can sign some of the best players and coaches in the world and maintain their top spot.

Defender Chris Smalling's power and quick thinking on the field give Manchester United constant protection in front of their goal.

Midfielder Ander Herrera has been playing for Manchester United since 2014.

MANCHESTER UNITED

Arena Old Trafford

Division English Premier League

Head Coach José Mourinho

Location Manchester, England

FIFA Club World Cups 1

Nicknames The Red Devils, United, Man U

19
Appearances in the Football Association Challenge (FA) Cup final

2
Team names

9–0
Largest Premier League win

76,098
Biggest Home Crowd

20.2 million
Instagram followers

History

At the beginning of the 1900s, Manchester United was running out of money. Luckily, a man named John Henry Davies agreed to invest in the team to help them pay their bills.

In 1878, a group of railway workers from the Lancashire and Yorkshire Railway (LYR) formed a soccer club. They called it Newton Heath LYR Football Club. At first, the team most often played other railway workers in friendly matches. Then, in 1892, they decided to enter the new English soccer league, called The English First Division. In 1902, they changed their name to Manchester United.

The team struggled to add wins to their scoresheet during the 1920s and 1930s. However, in the late 1940s, they soared to the top of English soccer. In 1958, a tragic event marked the team's history forever. On February 6, the team's plane crashed in Munich, Germany. Twenty-three people died and eight of them were players. Credit for rebuilding the team, physically and emotionally, goes to legendary coach Matt Busby. He helped lead the team back to the top ranks of the league by 1965.

Manchester United continued to have the winning formula during the 1990s and early 2000s. Their outstanding players and capable coaches kept the team atop the Premier League. The squad won the league title 13 times in 20 years.

Every year, on February 6th, fans come to Old Trafford to honor those who died in the Munich airplane crash. It has become a tradition to sing the song "The Flowers of Manchester." The song has been dedicated to those who died.

The Arena

Kids can have their **birthday parties** at Old Trafford stadium's Manchester United Red Café, complete with a visit from team mascot Fred the Red.

Old Trafford is the second largest stadium in the Premier League.

Manchester United has played on the Old Trafford stadium **pitch** since 1910. Before that, they spent time playing at two other fields in Manchester. Old Trafford was a big improvement from those fields, which were described as "mud heaps." The stadium held 80,000 people for its first game on February 19, 1910. During World War II (1939–1945), Old Trafford was bombed and partially destroyed. The stadium was repaired, and, by 1949, United were back on the pitch.

Old Trafford has gone through many renovations since its early days. The standing-room sections were converted to seating areas and second tiers were added to make room for more fans. A team museum was also built. Today, Old Trafford is considered a world-class arena. It has hosted several UEFA Champions League finals and FIFA World Cup tournament matches.

Star player Bobby Charlton called Old Trafford the "Theatre of Dreams," and the name stuck. Today, there is even a song with the same name.

Where They Play

SWEDEN

FINLAND

NORWAY

DENMARK

GERMANY

Arena
Old Trafford

Location
Manchester, England

Broke Ground
1909

Completed
February 19, 1910

Field Design
Large glass panels greet spectators at the entrance of the stadium. Occasionally, images are projected onto the glass, such as team photos or player tributes.

Features
- 75,643 seats
- Stadium tours with former players
- Manchester United Red Café

PREMIER LEAGUE TEAMS

1 Arsenal *(Holloway, London, England)*
2 Bournemouth *(Bournemouth, England)*
3 Brighton and Hove Albion *(Brighton and Hove, England)*
4 Burnley *(Burnley, England)*
5 Chelsea *(West London, England)*
6 Crystal Palace *(South London, England)*
7 Everton *(Liverpool, England)*
8 Huddersfield Town *(Huddersfield, England)*
9 Leicester City *(Leicester, England)*
10 Liverpool *(Liverpool, England)*
11 Manchester City *(Manchester, England)*
★ 12 Manchester United *(Manchester, England)*
13 Newcastle United *(Newcastle upon Tyne, England)*
14 Southampton *(Southampton, England)*
15 Stoke City *(Stoke-on-Trent, England)*
16 Swansea City *(Swansea, Wales)*
17 Tottenham Hotspur *(North London, England)*
18 Watford *(Watford, England)*
19 West Bromwich Albion *(West Bromwich, England)*
20 West Ham United *(East London, England)*

The Uniforms

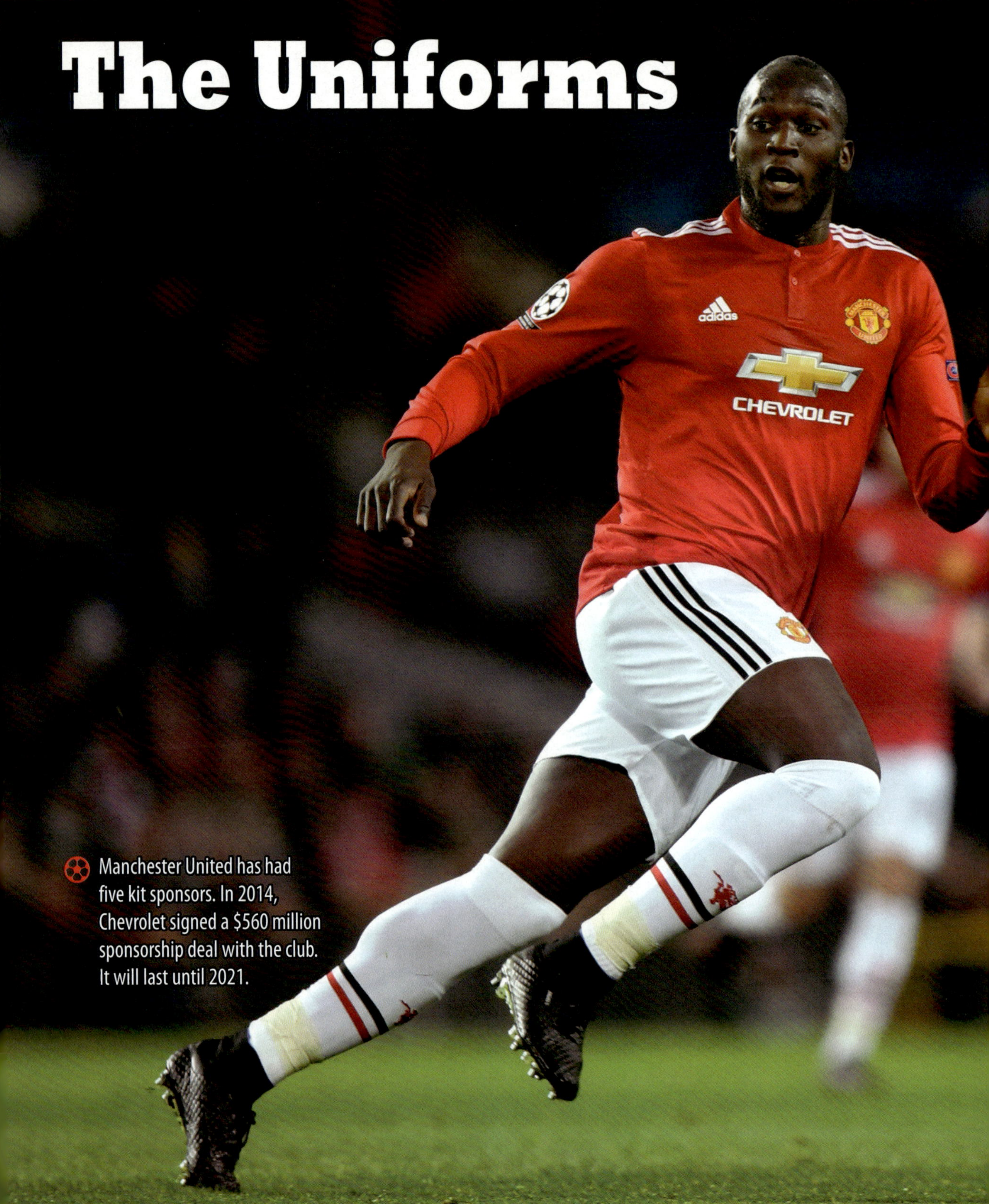

Manchester United has had five kit sponsors. In 2014, Chevrolet signed a $560 million sponsorship deal with the club. It will last until 2021.

HOME

Manchester United players are known for their red **kits**. However, they did not start out wearing the color. When the team was still called Newton Heath LYR, they wore green and gold jerseys. In 1902, they changed the team name to Manchester United and first used the color red for their kits.

Over time, the uniform style has changed, but red has remained constant. In recent years, the uniforms have had the name of a team **sponsor** in big letters across the front of the jersey. The name on the jersey changes every few years, depending on which company is sponsoring the team. For away games, Manchester United wears a black kit. Sometimes, if their jersey color is too similar to their opponent's jerseys, the team wears a third kit that is light gray with dark gray trim.

In 1996, Manchester United's gray jerseys became infamous when the team changed out of them after a losing first half against Southampton. Many fans believe they bring bad luck.

Goalie Gear

Current goalie David de Gea has been a powerful presence for United. Since joining the team in 2011, de Gea has appeared in goal 296 times.

The **goalkeeper** is the only Manchester United player at home games not wearing red. Keepers wear a different color than their teammates. This way, they are easily recognized as the goalkeeper. The Manchester United goalkeepers wear a dark blue kit. When they play away matches, the goalkeepers wear a bright green jersey.

Unlike other professional sports goalies, soccer keepers do not usually wear any special body padding or helmets. They are allowed to wear gloves to protect their hands. The gloves also give them additional grip when handling the ball.

Peter Schmeichel is considered one of the best goalkeepers Manchester United has ever had. He defended the goal for United in 398 matches before moving on to Portugal's Sporting CP in 1999. While he was with United, the 6 foot 4 inch (193 centimeters) goalkeeper helped the team capture the Premier League title five times.

In 1993, Peter Schmeichel was the Manchester United goalkeeper during the FA Charity Shield at Wembley Stadium. In the competition, United beat Arsenal 5–4 on penalties.

The Coaches

Current coach José Mourinho is the first coach in Manchester United history to win a major title in his first season with the team.

There are two coaches in Manchester United's long history who stand out from the rest: Matt Busby and Alex Ferguson. These coaches stayed with the team for more than 20 years each. They guided the players to dozens of league titles, cups, and championships. Loved by players and fans, they devoted their lives to United. Queen Elizabeth II even **knighted** them as a tribute to their service to English soccer.

ALEX FERGUSON In his 26 years with United, Alex Ferguson helped the team dominate the English Premier League. His crowning accomplishment came in 1999. That year, he led the team to their first "**treble**," winning the Premier League championship, the FA Cup, and the UEFA Champions League.

MATT BUSBY Matt Busby served the team for 24 years, from 1945 to 1969. Not only did he survive the 1958 plane crash, he also brought the shattered team back together. Busby led the team to five English league wins and two FA Cup titles. His squad of successful young players was nicknamed the "Busby Babes."

JOSÉ MOURINHO José Mourinho is the current coach for Manchester United. He is new to the team, but is certainly not new to professional soccer. Mourinho arrived in 2016 after successful stints at Chelsea, Real Madrid, and Benfica, among others. His impact on United was immediate. In his first season, he led the team to be victors of the UEFA Europa League.

Fans Around the World

As a salute to fans, Manchester United players take a "lap of honor" around the field after the final home match of each season.

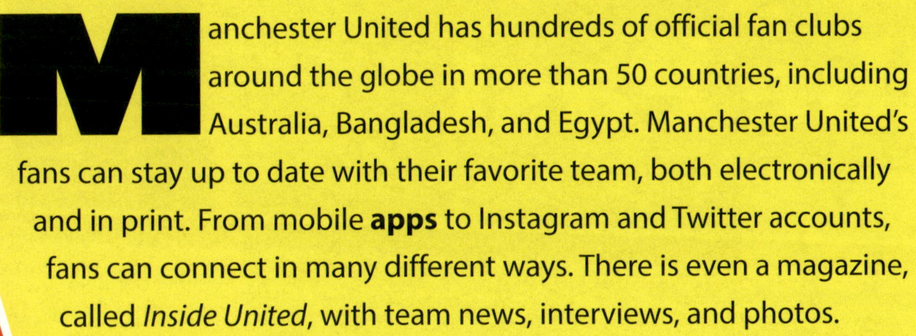

Manchester United has hundreds of official fan clubs around the globe in more than 50 countries, including Australia, Bangladesh, and Egypt. Manchester United's fans can stay up to date with their favorite team, both electronically and in print. From mobile **apps** to Instagram and Twitter accounts, fans can connect in many different ways. There is even a magazine, called *Inside United*, with team news, interviews, and photos.

The team has more than 70 million followers on their Facebook page. United's fans are known for the many songs and chants they sing during home and away games. Some of the songs include "We Love United," "Hello Hello We Are the Busby Boys," and "When the Reds Go Marching In."

Fan Traditions

#1 Mascot Fred the Red roams the stadium, encouraging the crowd to sing, dance, and cheer on the team.

#2 A fan favorite to sing at each game is "Glory, Glory, Man United," sung to the tune of "The Battle Hymn of the Republic."

Legends of the Past

Many great players have suited up for Manchester United. A few of them have become icons of the team and the city it represents.

Position: Forward
Years in Pro Soccer: 1956–1976
Born: October 11, 1937, Ashington, England

Bobby Charlton

Forward Bobby Charlton is known as the most successful player ever to play for Manchester United. In his 758 games, he dominated the pitch. He scored 249 times, a team record that held until 2017. Charlton is remembered for his determination and leadership during Manchester United's difficult rebuilding years. He led the way for United to take home three Premier League championships and one FA Cup. In 1966, Charlton was named Footballer of the Year and European Player of the Year. He was knighted by Queen Elizabeth II, and he went on to write several books about his years as a soccer player.

Ryan Giggs

Ryan Giggs was known for his expert passing and goal-scoring abilities. His long career, played exclusively with Manchester United, spanned 23 years. During that time, he collected 13 Premier League championships and four FA Cups. Giggs was part of Alex Ferguson's powerhouse team that brought home the treble in 1999. In 2012, Giggs was a member of Great Britain's soccer team at the London Summer Olympics. After wrapping up his days on the pitch in 2014 and moving into coaching, Giggs was awarded with Manchester United's Lifetime Achievement Award.

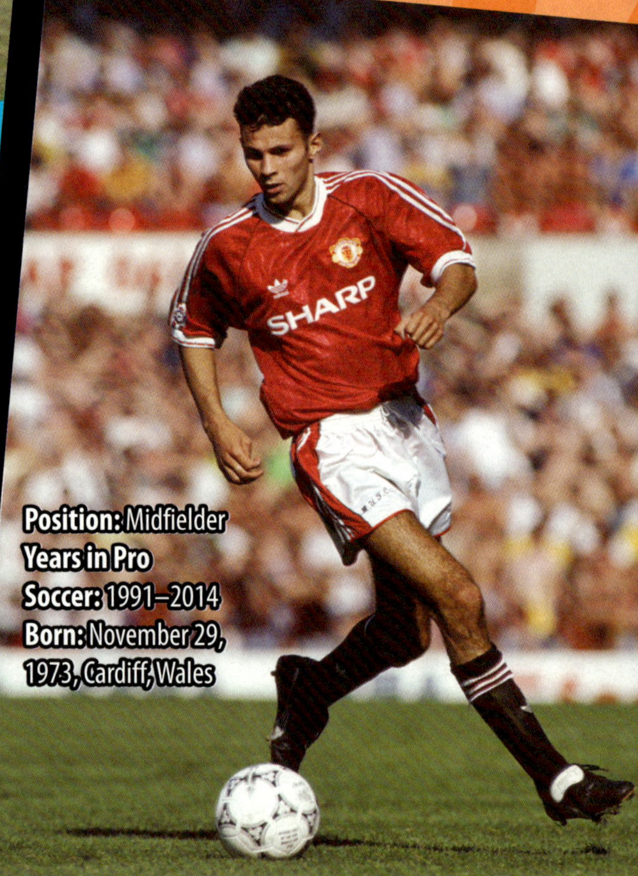

Position: Midfielder
Years in Pro Soccer: 1991–2014
Born: November 29, 1973, Cardiff, Wales

Paul Scholes

Paul Scholes spent his entire career with United. He made his mark as one of the best players the team has ever had. Scholes was known for his passing precision and his ability to find the net from any distance. The midfielder is one of the most decorated players in team history. He helped Manchester United bring home an amazing 11 Premier League titles. In his 718 appearances, the third highest in club history, he scored 155 times. Scholes was also part of the 1999 super squad that captured the all-important treble.

Position: Midfielder
Years in Pro Soccer: 1994–2013
Born: November 16, 1974, Salford, England

George Best

George Best joined Manchester United in 1963. He was just 17. He went on to become a key ingredient in coach Matt Busby's dream team with Denis Law and Bobby Charlton. Best was known for his speed, balance, and unmatched ball control. He used those skills to help the team bring home the Premier League championship in 1965, and again in 1967. A goal by Best in the 1968 European Cup final led the team to victory, and the cup came to Manchester for the first time. He was awarded the 1968 Ballon d'Or, an annual award for outstanding performance.

Position: Forward
Years in Pro Soccer: 1963–1983
Born: May 22, 1946, Belfast, Northern Ireland

Stars of Today

Today's Manchester United team is made up of many young, talented players who have proven that they are among the best in the league.

Juan Mata

Juan Mata moved to Manchester United from Chelsea in 2014. In March 2015, he scored a goal against Liverpool with an overhead kick that made him an immediate fan favorite. The 5 foot 7 inch (170 cm) midfielder has scored 39 goals in his 169 appearances. He has helped United win the FA Cup and the Premier League Cup. Mata's outstanding play-making skills and passing precision make him a valuable asset on the Manchester squad. He also plays for his home country of Spain in World Cup competitions and was part of the Spanish team that competed in the 2012 Olympics.

Position: Midfielder
Years in Pro Soccer: 2006–present
Born: April 28, 1988, Burgos, Spain

David de Gea

David de Gea joined the squad in 2011 from the Spanish soccer league's Atlético Madrid. De Gea's imposing height and swift reflexes make him a powerful force in goal. He helped the team win the Premier League championship in 2013 and the FA Cup in 2016. He is the only player in Manchester United history to be honored with the **Sir Matt Busby Player of the Year** award for three **consecutive** years. De Gea also lends his goalkeeping skill to Spain's national team in international competition.

Position: Goalkeeper
Years in Pro Soccer: 2009–present
Born: November 7, 1990, Madrid, Spain

Paul Pogba

Known for his crazy hairstyles, Paul Pogba started his career in the Manchester United youth league. He then played for Juventus in the Italian soccer league. Finally, he came back to Manchester United in 2016. His energy, dribbling ability, and technical skills set him apart from other players. The 6 foot 3 inch (191 cm) midfielder also plays for France's national team. He was honored with the FIFA Young Player Award for his 2014 World Cup performance. There, he scored a goal in a match against Nigeria that helped France win 2–0.

Position: Midfielder
Years in Pro Soccer: 2011–present
Born: March 15, 1993, Lagny-sur-Marne, France

Anthony Martial

Anthony Martial started off his career in Manchester as the team's top scorer. He scored 17 goals during the 2015–16 season, and won the club's Goal of the Season award for a goal against Liverpool. In his short time with Manchester United, the 6 foot (183 cm) forward has scored 34 goals in 121 matches. He has also helped the team bring home the Premier League cup in 2017 and the FA Cup in 2016. Martial is known for his incredible speed, technical skills, and goal-scoring ability.

Position: Forward
Years in Pro Soccer: 2013–present
Born: December 5, 1995, Massy, France

All-Time Records

253
Goals Scored
Wayne Rooney has the record for scoring the most goals for the Reds, beating out Bobby Charlton by just four.

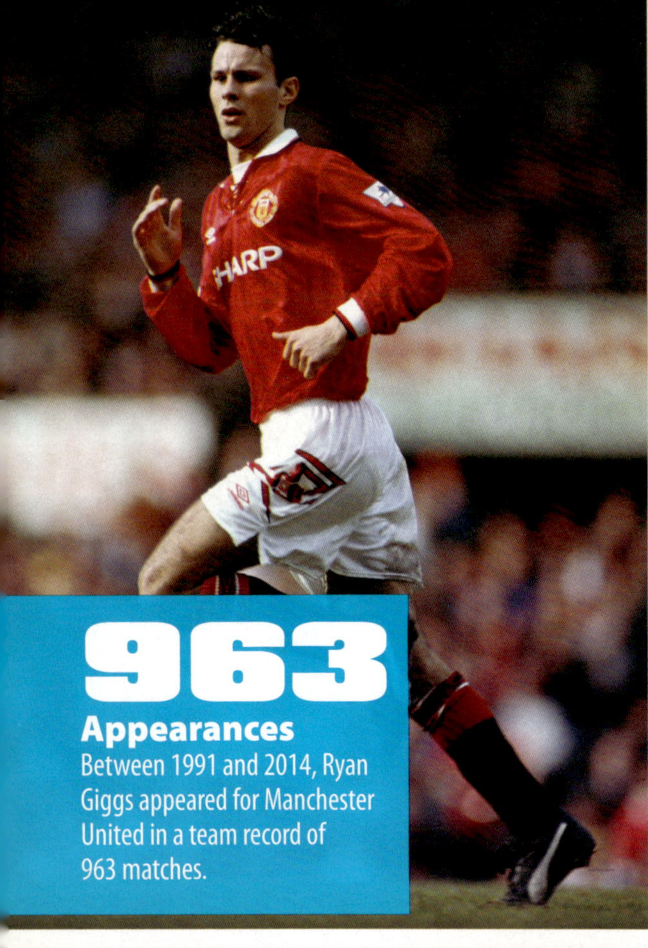

963
Appearances
Between 1991 and 2014, Ryan Giggs appeared for Manchester United in a team record of 963 matches.

18
Hat Tricks
During the team's successful run in the 1960s, Denis Law contributed 18 **hat tricks** to United.

20
Premier League championships
Manchester United holds the record for most Premier League championships, ahead of second-place Liverpool's 18.

5
Goals in a Match
Andy Cole made Manchester's record books when he scored five goals in a match against Ipswich Town in 1995.

Timeline

Throughout the team's history, Manchester United has had many memorable events that have become defining moments for the team and its fans.

1878
Railway workers at the Lancashire and Yorkshire Railway (LYR) start a soccer team called Newton Heath LYR.

1945
Matt Busby joins Manchester United as coach.

1902
The team changes their name to Manchester United.

1890 · 1900 · 1910 · 1920 · 1930 · 1940 · 1950

In 1908, The new team wins their first soccer league title.

1910
The team plays their first game at Old Trafford stadium in front of 80,000 spectators.

1958
The team's plane crashes in Munich, Germany, killing 23 people, including 8 players.

1999
For the first time ever, the team wins the treble. Celtic is the only other team in the United Kingdom to have achieved this honor.

The Future
Manchester United has its sights set on bringing the Premier League title back home to Old Trafford, a title they have not won since 2013. With their squad of strong young players, an experienced coaching staff, and fiercely loyal fans, the team is ready to compete for years to come.

1960 1970 1980 1990 2000 2010 2020

1986
Alex Ferguson joins Manchester United as coach.

In 1994, the squad wins both the Premier League championship and the FA Cup.

April 2016
The 1,000th Manchester United Premier League goal at Old Trafford is scored by Anthony Martial.

Write a Biography

Life Story

A person's life story can be the subject of a book. This kind of book is called a biography. Biographies often describe the lives of people who have achieved great success. These people may be alive today, or they may have lived many years ago. Reading a biography can help you learn more about a great person.

Get the Facts

Use this book, and research in the library and on the internet, to find out more about your favorite player. Learn as much about him as you can. What position does he play? What are his statistics in important categories? Has he set any records? Also, be sure to write down key events in the person's life. What was his childhood like? What has he accomplished off the field? Is there anything else that makes this person special or unusual?

Use the Concept Web

A concept web is a useful research tool. Read the questions in the concept web on the following page. Answer the questions in your notebook. Your answers will help you write a biography.

Concept Web

Your Opinion

- What did you learn from the books you read in your research?
- Would you suggest these books to others?
- Was anything missing from these books?

Adulthood

- Where does this individual currently reside?
- Does he or she have a family?

Childhood

- Where and when was this person born?
- Describe his or her parents, siblings, and friends.
- Did this person grow up in unusual circumstances?

Accomplishments off the Field

- What is this person's life's work?
- Has he or she received awards or recognition for accomplishments?
- How have this person's accomplishments served others?

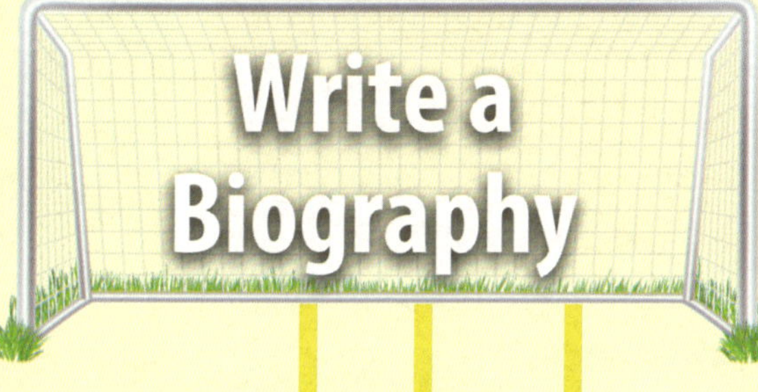

Help and Obstacles

- Did this individual have a positive attitude?
- Did he or she receive help from others?
- Did this person have a mentor?
- Did this person face any hardships?
- If so, how were the hardships overcome?

Accomplishments on the Field

- What records does this person hold?
- What key games and plays have defined his career?
- What are his stats in categories important to his position?

Work and Preparation

- What was this person's education?
- What was his or her work experience?
- How does this person work?
- What is the process he or she uses?

Trivia Time

Take this quiz to test your knowledge of Manchester United. The answers are printed upside down under each question.

1 What was Manchester United's first name?

A. Newton Heath LYR

2 What is the name of the team's stadium?

A. Old Trafford

3 How many years was Alex Ferguson Manchester's coach?

A. 26

4 How many Premier League championships has the team won?

A. 20

5 In what year did United win the treble?

A. 1999

6 Who is the team's top scorer?

A. Wayne Rooney

7 Who was named the Sir Matt Busby Player of the Year for three straight years?

A. David de Gea

8 What position did Bobby Charlton play?

A. Forward

9 What song is a fan favorite to be sung each game?

A. "Glory, Glory Man United"

Key Words

apps: computer programs that perform special functions

consecutive: following one after another in a series

cups: trophies, and in some cases, the names of actual competitions

forward: a player on a soccer team who normally plays closest to the opponent's goal

goalkeeper: also called a goalie. The player responsible for keeping the ball from going into the goal and the only player who is allowed to pick up the ball.

hat tricks: three goals scored by one player in a game

kits: the standard attire and equipment worn by soccer players, including a shirt, shorts, socks, and shin guards

knighted: to be given a special honor and the title of Sir by the king or queen of England

pitch: an area that is used for playing sports

Sir Matt Busby Player of the Year: the award given to a player on Manchester United who is voted by fans as the best player of the year

sponsor: a company that contributes to the costs of a sports team in exchange for the right to advertise

trebles: having won three major trophies in a single sports season or calendar year

Index

Log on to www.av2books.com

AV² by Weigl brings you media enhanced books that support active learning. Go to www.av2books.com, and enter the special code found on page 2 of this book. You will gain access to enriched and enhanced content that supplements and complements this book. Content includes video, audio, weblinks, quizzes, a slide show, and activities.

AV² Online Navigation

Audio
Listen to sections of the book read aloud.

Book Pages
AV² pages directly correspond to pages in the book.

Video
Watch informative video clips.

Embedded Weblinks
Gain additional information for research.

Key Words
Study vocabulary, and complete a matching word activity.

Try This!
Complete activities and hands-on experiments.

Quizzes
Test your knowledge.

Slide Show
View images and captions, and prepare a presentation.

AV² was built to bridge the gap between print and digital. We encourage you to tell us what you like and what you want to see in the future.

Sign up to be an AV² Ambassador at www.av2books.com/ambassador.

Due to the dynamic nature of the Internet, some of the URLs and activities provided as part of AV² by Weigl may have changed or ceased to exist. AV² by Weigl accepts no responsibility for any such changes. All media enhanced books are regularly monitored to update addresses and sites in a timely manner. Contact AV² by Weigl at 1-866-649-3445 or av2books@weigl.com with any questions, comments, or feedback.